MW01625956

My Dearest Fran: 5.28.2013
So very glad to have you in my life. You are a treat for the heart and soul.
May this book helps you harness the power of anger with more and grace.
Blessings!
MG

TRILOGY OF ANGER

{COMMUNICATION AIKIDO:}

Take Back *Your* Power with Boundaries, Expectations and Skill

MARGARITA GURRI, PH.D.

Curchy Publishing Group
Melbourne, FL

Curchy Publishing Group
Melbourne, FL 32907

Edited by Steve Lee
Cover by Caley Curchy

ISBN: 978-0-615-72619-9
LCCN: 34187688
CreateSpace, North Charleston, SC

For further information please contact:
DMG@DrGurri.com
855-DrGurri (374-8774)

Published 2012 Curchy Publishing Group
Printed in the USA

{ *Peace begins with a smile.*
~ Mother Teresa ~ }

COMMUNICATION AIKIDO:

is all about fostering our personal power in the way we think about and handle our response to anger, in others and ourselves.

⁂

BOOK I
Three Levels of Anger

Ever been angered by stupid? Use the principles of the martial art of Aikido to invite each of us to react to others' anger and negative input productively in a creative and positive way. It's just so easy to become grumpy or unpleasant when faced with life's stressors.

⁂

BOOK II
Tao of Poo

Poo happens. What do you do about it? Learn to use humor in the face of anger and crisis. Sharpen your use of nonverbal and verbal communication skills. Like Arnold Schwarzenegger in *Kindergarten Cop*, everyone wishes they could shut-up some folks. Learn to do this graciously, with quiet and more direct leadership.

⁂

BOOK III
Polite Shut-ups

Tired of rude? Want to set limits graciously? Polite Shut-ups are the answer. They are simple, fun limit-setting strategies that anyone can master. With a sense of humor, some communication skills, and kindness, you can be a master of Polite Shut-ups.

Contents

BOOK II
Tao of Poo

⁂

BOOK III
Polite Shut-ups

If you lean into or away from anger, you get hit or lose your personal power. If you harness anger – leadership, creativity and tranquility bloom.

~ Margarita Gurri, Ph.D. ~

To everyone who has ever made anyone angry.
You know who you are. Thanks!

and to...

Daughters, Jess Ennis and Kate Gurri Glass;
Granddaughters, Taryn and Kaitlyn Ennis;
Twin sister, Elena Gurri;
Siblings, Joe Gurri and Irene Gurri;
Friends, Danny Oropesa, Ed Dunkelblau, Chip Lutz,
Tony Palm, Janis Chinnock Wetter and Paul Wetter;
Artist, Caley Curchy;
Editor, Steve Lee; and
Parents, Joseph and Beba Gurri.

and then ...

Thanks to Dennis Jonio, for his gentle and pushy support in getting these thoughts onto these pages, at last!

⁂

Funny is certainly all around me.
ENJOY!

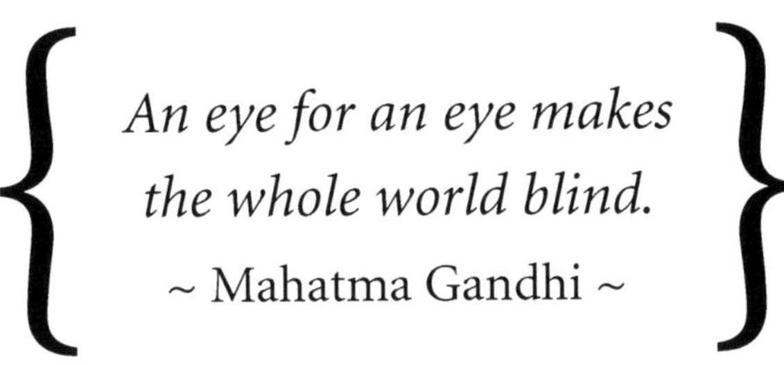

An eye for an eye makes
the whole world blind.

~ Mahatma Gandhi ~

Foreword

By Steve Lee, Editor

Trilogy of Anger's Communication Aikido: Take Back *Your* Power with Boundaries, Expectations and Skill is the first book authored by Margarita Gurri, Ph.D., but it is definitely not the last. Fittingly, readers will be clamoring for more anecdotes and wisdom from the good doctor once they have finished her inaugural publication.

A licensed psychologist, consultant, speaker and author — Margarita is all that and more as you will discern while reading her book. She also is a family matriarch, loving mother and wife. Margarita is passionate about helping families, youth and military personnel get through tough times and promoting a lifetime of togetherness.

Plus, she is a black belt in karate, hence Communication Aikido.

A keen sense of humor and sharp wit are balanced by 30 years of professional expertise. It all adds up to an uncanny ability to deliver informative solutions to life's problems in an easily discernible manner to her readers. Those traits are apparent throughout Trilogy of Anger, which represents her initial foray into the publishing business.

A refugee from Castro's Cuba who arrived on U.S. soil during the turbulent 1960s, Margarita relies on her own experiences and strength of character to share so much of herself with the families and people she has helped as a clinical psychologist. Whether she is dealing with individuals or families in an office environment, speaking to large groups at conferences and workshops or imparting her advice on the airwaves, Margarita's wisdom and compassion shine through.

So sit back and take your time to truly absorb the Trilogy of Anger. Margarita would like nothing more for you to make it a learning experience that will help you deal with situations — some tougher than others — that are all around us. She knows you'll be better for having read it, not to mention having a hearty laugh at some of her anecdotes along the way.

Jesus Has a Great Right Hook!

> *"I'm sorry you made me hit you!"*
> ~ Daughters Jess Ennis and
> Kate Gurri Glass ~
> *(when they were little)*

Inside each of us is the potential to be wonderful and awful. Each everyday moment is full of possibilities. Some moments feel yucky, some yummy. It's really all the same in terms of potential. It's up to us to recognize these experiences as gifts. What matters is how we respond in thought, word and deed.

COMMUNICATION AIKIDO

Sometimes a fun image helps us respond differently when it counts most. Never is this more obvious than when we are facing big emotions. Anger, although rarely the first emotional response for most of us, is the emotion we are most likely to identify as something that needs handling. Communication Aikido is all about a way to think about and handle our response to anger, in others and ourselves.

The idea of Aikido is to lead the attacker, using his or her own aggressive momentum in a way that no one is harmed. A Japanese martial art developed by Morihei Ueshiba, "Aikido" means "the way" or the method of unifying your life energy. The attacker's energy is redirected instead of being blocked or stopped.

Two stories best describe what led me to create Communication Aikido. The first story set the stage for me to pay attention to anger responses- others and mine. The second story describes the creation of the Three Levels of Anger and the follow up strategies of the Tao of Poo and Polite Shut-ups.

STORY ONE: **JESUS HAS A GREAT RIGHT HOOK!**

I began noticing how people deal with anger out of self-preservation. I came to this country from Cuba as a 4-year old refugee with my mother, twin sister Elena, older siblings Joe and Irene. We joined our father in Miami as he had left Cuba a few days earlier in November 1960. We left with a suitcase for the entire family and $5 per person. We moved into a very modest neighborhood and got mixed reviews in the welcome department.

Some folks were warm and inviting. A few were outright hostile. Most of these were kids who eagerly told us that they "hated" us because we did not speak English and looked different. They had heard confusing things about us. Some thought we were Communists, not refugees escaping Communism. Either way, I got beat up a few times. This got my attention. I learned to be fast, funny, and to notice others, my surroundings and myself.

When I came home crying, my mother would kiss the boo-boos or "ya-yas" (in Spanish) and treat any of the little injuries to the body or bigger ones of the heart. She suggested that we think of the bully as if he was Jesus and treat the bully as we would Jesus. Big task.

Man, did Jesus have a great right hook!

Mom calmly told us that since this was Jesus, we had a great opportunity to teach and to learn. "Show them who you are," Mom said. My mother, Beba, was a woman of simple and strong faith. Her faith was practical and showed itself in little everyday things.

After any incident, wonderful or awful, my mother would ask:

1. "What did you teach?"
2. "What did you learn?"

STORY TWO: **THE OCTAGON**

Angry First Responders. Ages ago, I was asked to consult with first responders who had soaked up the aggression and stress from their jobs and had become aggressive and unpleasant. Police officers, police chiefs, a fire chief and emergency medical technicians met with me in a small group for Anger Management. Nothing I did worked. After the second week, I went home a bit deflated. I was determined to create a way to help these nerve-frayed and temper-strong responders turn things around.

The idea of the Three Levels of Anger came to me when my children were young and I was ironing their clothes for the next day while watching TV. Two martial arts movies got me to thinking.

Chuck Norris, The Octagon. On the TV was one of my heroes, martial artist Chuck Norris, who was fully engaged in action-packed and philosophical problem solving in his movie The Octagon. Norris, always the last man standing, prevailed because he would not allow his temper to taint his response to even the most stunning attacks.

David Carradine, Circle of Iron. Another movie inspired by Bruce Lee Circle of Iron, originally known as The Silent Flute, is a morality play about life's choices. Although not a good choice in real life, the hero played by David Carradine wisely chooses to destroy a beautiful boy's face, clearly a counter-intuitive response.

By breaking the boy's nose, the boy is relieved of the burden and temptation of his own beauty and could now buckle down to work. Carradine's character explains that the boy was "too beautiful. He was a tyrant. He would have grown up to be worse. I freed his parents from the bondage of his beauty. … I freed his parents and the boy, too."

As I was watching, I got to thinking about my children and patients from my psychology practice. It's just so easy to get angry when someone is angry with us. It's easy to sink to their level and respond automatically in ways that are less than lovely.

* * *

THREE LEVELS OF ANGER ARE BORN

So, the Three Levels of Anger were born. The complete title is The Three Levels of Power in the Face of Anger, but that's just too long.

As I see it, there are three levels of anger or of power in the face of anger. The most primitive, reactive level is Level Three. The most common response is Level Two. The most sophisticated, enlightened response is Level One.

I'll introduce you to The Three Levels of Anger and some practical tools after inviting you to see where you are.

Let's see how you do.

BOOK I
THREE LEVELS OF ANGER

Three Levels of Anger

Humor is the great thing, the saving thing. The minute it crops up, all our irritation and resentments slip away, and a sunny spirit takes their place."
~ Mark Twain ~

The Three Levels of Anger, or the Three Levels of Power in the Face of Anger, is a fun way of looking at how we keep or give away our power.

HUMOR

Dealing with anger, theirs or ours, can be a serious business. Even so, humor really helps each of us to keep a light spirit and dust off our funny bone. Mark Twain said it best, "Humor is the great thing, the saving thing. The minute it crops up, all our irritation and resentments slip away, and a sunny spirit takes their place."

So, keep in mind that humor is all around you. Humor helps us be creative in our view of situations, helps us deal with stress, heal, laugh and be more productive.

PERSONAL POWER

With Personal Power and Humor, we can all achieve the First Level of Anger.

Personal power is all about knowing who we are, how we influence others, and how they influence us. It's about responsibility, self-awareness and grace in challenging times. This book is all about maintaining and cultivating our personal power in the best of times and the worst of times. (Just can't help but think of Charles Dickens when I think about personal power).

It grows from self-awareness, emotional and social awareness, acceptance of our responsibility and blame, and impeccability with the truth about us, others and the world around us. For a great discussion of impeccability, I suggest you read Don Miguel Ruiz's The Four Agreements.

LIFE'S CHALLENGES AS BLESSINGS

Back when I discovered that Jesus had a great right hook, remember the two insightful and annoying questions my mother asked. With each yucky or yummy event we can ask ourselves:

1. **"What did I learn?"**
2. **"What did I teach?"**

Three Levels of Anger Paradigm

"It's not my fault you made me hit you!"
~ Anonymous ~
(but could be any four-year old anywhere)

RESPONSE LEVEL	THIRD LEVEL OF ANGER	SECOND LEVEL OF ANGER	FIRST LEVEL OF ANGER
The Action	I hit. You hit.	I hit. You don't hit. You get distracted and have a delayed, diluted reaction against yourself or others.	I hit. You don't hit. You show compassion for self and others.
Who Wins? Motorcycle	I win. Get on the back.	I win. Get on the back.	You win. You ride.
Goal	Promote violence, attitude, and share grumpy moods.	Self-preservation.	World peace.
Response	⟷ Same Same	↲↑ Same Sideways	○ Same Tranquil-Compassionate
Energy	Returned in the same or escalated manner.	Turns sideways and becomes a delayed time bomb.	Passes without harm to self or other. Power is retained and strengthened.
Typified by	Jerry Springer Show participants	Polite Folk Anywhere	Yoda (Star Wars™)

⁂

THIRD LEVEL of Anger

[*Jerry Springer Show participants*
I slap you]

Please take a moment to think or to jot down some thoughts. Answering quickly helps us see where we really are right here, right now.

- What do you do?
- How do you feel?
- What do you think?

How'd you do?

You are a member of the Jerry Springer Show, a bona-fide Level Three responder.

"Jerry, Jerry, Jerry!"

I slap you, you slap me right back. I call you a name, you call me something worse. You throw a chair, jump me and call Steve to attack or subdue me, get the audience on your side and say, "He's not the daddy!" Violence and ill moods abound. Anger begets anger.

WHO WINS? WHO'S IN CHARGE?

In the civilized world no one wins when we resort to violence. I've asked these questions to audiences and workshop participants all over the United States. Answers vary from:

- "The slapped one is in charge since they didn't start the violence" to
- "No one is in charge where violence exists" to
- "The person who hit the hardest is in charge."

In my way of thinking, I am in charge. In the world of domination and control, I win. I hit and made you hit me back. Because of my actions, you lost your focus. Right? Well, it's not so easy.

Eleanor Roosevelt said it best, "No one can make you feel inferior without your consent." No one can make you mad, either. It's up to you. Level Three is good practice in understanding how we each give away our power to others.

Have you noticed that someone can ruin your day with just a look? What power we give to that person! Often that look-giver isn't even that important to us. No healthy person wants others to think of him or her in a yucky way or be treated badly. As we mature, we deal with this natural response and give it it's proper due. Only certain people's opinion of us really matters. It's up to us to choose our own responses and our advisors wisely. If everyone approves of us, we are doing something really wrong.

In Level Three, the most primitive level of response to others and ourselves, we forget our own tranquility and values to go straight into automatic same-same response mode. I bullied or startled you into changing your path. I own you. I influenced you off your agenda to mine. I hit, you hit. The energy goes directly from me to you. I win.

LEVEL THREE OF THE THREE LEVELS OF ANGER PARADIGM

MOTORCYCLE:	If we were on a Harley Davidson, you'd be on the back. You know what that makes you! Get on the back of my motorcycle. I own you.
GOAL:	The goal of a Level Three response to anger is to promote violence, attitude, and share grumpy moods.
RESPONSE:	Same ⟷ Same
ENERGY:	The energy is returned in the same or in an escalated manner.

SECOND LEVEL of Anger

Polite Folk Anywhere

I slap you.
You don't slap me.

WHAT WOULD MOST POLITE FOLK DO?

The Second Level of Anger is exemplified by most polite folk. I hit you. You are more sophisticated and refrain from hitting me back or hurling insults my way.

What would you do?

Most people say they would say:

- "Hey, why'd you hit me?" in a whiny offended tone
- Do nothing
- Call the cops
- Shake their heads and "tsk" at me
- Most would stammer
- Avoid a response
- Some would even apologize for getting in the way or for inviting a slap, while
- Others would just complain

WHAT HAPPENS TO POLITE FOLK LATER IN THE DAY?

They get a tummy ache, headache, get whiny, grumpy, kick the dog, scold the child, spend too much money, drink too much, gamble recklessly on money or safety, eat too much or too little, sleep too much or too little, exercise too much or too little, self-medicate with a preferred substance, have great sex but with the wrong partner or no sex with the right one. The list goes on.

Polite Folk are the bread and butter of any psychology or medical practice. Stress responses in the face of impotent anger or rage attacks our souls and bodies. It's not a pretty sight.

You are too sophisticated to react automatically with an immediate and transparent return of violence. The energy does not go directly from me to you. It goes from me to you sideways, like a delayed-action time bomb. The anger I sent your way is not returned directly, it goes sideways, so that later that day you kick the dog, yell at a loved one, eat too much, sleep too little, have great sex but with the wrong partner, gamble, spend too much money, etc.

The ways we react in Level Two are the common ones in the realm of anxiety, mild depression, passive aggression, and mild self-destructive behavior fueled by swallowing our anger.

WHO WINS? WHO'S IN CHARGE?

Again, I do. I made you lose your tranquility and took power from you. Although the anger is not the same as I dished out, I made you lose your tranquility and get off your path of the day to react to my aggressive slap and your passive, polite reaction. Of course, I did this with your full permission, but you give me all the credit.

Sweet!

LEVEL TWO OF THE THREE LEVELS OF ANGER PARADIGM

MOTORCYCLE:	Again, get on the back of the motorcycle. You are mine.
GOAL:	The goal of a Level Two response is self-preservation. At best we offer passive assistance in the form of prayers and gracious thoughts. At worst we are judgmental.
RESPONSE:	Same ↵↑ Sideways
ENERGY:	The energy is turned sideways and becomes like a delayed time bomb, exploding or imploding over time at indirect targets. We kick the dog, yell at our partner, honk at slightly slow drivers, etc.

⁂

FIRST LEVEL of Anger

[

Yoda (Star Wars™)

Now, we get to Yoda. You are a sophisticated Level One responder.

I hit you.

OOOOMMMMMM!

You don't hit me back.

]

YOU don't surrender your tranquility to me. You don't slap back as in the Jerry Springer mode. You don't just passively take it while it eats you up like in Polite Folk mode. You ask two questions.

TWO QUESTIONS

One of me and one of you.

1. **For me the Slapper:**
   - Why did you hit me? ("Hit me, why did you, hmm." – in Yoda-speak)
2. **For you as Yoda:**
   - What did I do to contribute to this slap?

FIRST LEVEL OF ANGER, QUESTION ONE:

What questions would you ask me, the slapper?

Yep:

- Why did you hit me… or
- Hit me, why did you (in Yoda-speak)?

How can you tell if you or another person is too angry to have a useful conversation? It's not always wise to ask a violent person in a rage a why question or anything. Please take a look to the Drink of Water Test for guidance in making this decision (See the following section). It's as simple as one, two, three.

FIRST LEVEL OF ANGER, QUESTION TWO:

What did I do to contribute to this slap?

Think. What question do you ask yourself?

The second question, you as Yoda asks: "What did I do to contribute to this slap?" If nothing, fine. If you contributed, take full accountability. This is a question of responsibility and true contribution.

Responsibility. Did you do anything to contribute to the act of me hitting you? Anything recent, past, accidental or on purpose? Fess up to yourself. Be aware of being too guilty and assuming too much guilt when there is none. Too often we blame ourselves for others' actions. If only I hadn't... If only I had.

As my mother used to say to me, "You are not a bus driver. You don't have to pick up everyone at every stop." She was talking about the importance of boundaries and not rescuing people - to let people take care of themselves with or without our support. Taking on too much guilt is just as destructive as avoiding our true guilt.

Folks that are overly guilty ask, "How did I cause this?" This is a dangerous way to think about others and ourselves. It's best to think about contributions more neutrally to see how everyone and environmental factors contributed to the slap. We'll discuss this in the Event Autopsy section below.

Be truthful. Be impeccable in your truth.

If you did contribute to my slapping you, take responsibility. Apologize to me or to yourself. Make plans to make amends. Step up. Be brave. Be strong. This is not always easy to do. We are all just so awesome and awful, often at the same time.

Even if you didn't contribute to getting slapped, a Level One response invites thoughts, feelings and behavior offering compassion for the slapper. Get out of my way. Do not allow me to hit you, but decide if any action is required to ensure my safety, your own safety, and the safety of others in my path. What to do? We'll talk about this in a later chapter. Let's practice.

WHO WINS?

You do. Ta da!

This is the only truly enlightened, empowered, world-saving response. You take my anger and violence, maintain your own tranquility and values, and contribute positively and thoughtfully with your energy and intentions.

Congratulations, you are one of the few in our world who can rise above the tempting hate and seductive negative energy to lead and heal. Thanks!

LEVEL ONE OF THE THREE LEVELS OF ANGER PARADIGM

MOTORCYCLE:	At last, you are on the motorcycle as a proud rider. Or you chose not to ride the bike. It's clear that you have the power to make this your choice. You are your own person.
GOAL:	World Peace. Level Three responders seek to show love and compassion to themselves and others.
RESPONSE:	Same ○ Tranquil-Compassionate
ENERGY:	The energy passes by without harming them or us. Ta Da! You have maintained and strengthened your personal power and provided an opportunity for healthy responses form the unsteady slapper.

SUMMARY

Communication Aikido is about responding to our own and others' yucky energy and behavioral responses with our personal power intact, so that we remain true to ourselves. Only at the First Level of Power do we retain and strengthen our power in the face of anger and annoyance, ours and theirs.

Some tools help us achieve Communication Aikido with clarity and skill. A few of these are: Drink of Water Test, Tao of Poo and Polite Shut-ups.

Drink of Water Test

{ *Nothing useful comes from talking with someone too mad to accept and drink a glass of water.*
~ Anonymous ~ (*Johns Hopkins Hospital Shock Trauma Nurse)* }

Many years ago, a nurse from the Johns Hopkins Hospital Shock Trauma Unit told me of a simple, elegant way of deciding if it's "safe" to talk in the face of anger, ours or theirs. It's an exercise in decision-making.

DRINK OF WATER TEST: READINESS TO TALK IN THE FACE OF ANGER

Imagine offering me, the angry slapping person, a full glass of water. I've broken down the Drink of Water Test into three easy steps.

1. **Step One: Your Readiness**
If you can pour water in the glass, and offer it to me without spilling, spitting or throwing it at the angry me, you are ready to talk. Sometimes we add to the tension without knowing it, sometimes we add to it on purpose. Anger is so amazingly contagious and irresistible at times, it can be more seductive than chocolate!

2. **Step Two: My Readiness**
If the angry me can reach for the offered glass of water, grasp it, bring it to my mouth, drink, and swallow without spilling a drop or throwing it at you at each step of the way, I am fit for discussion, too.

3. **Step Three: Our Readiness**
If one drop spills or is choked on or thrown by either party, allow some time for that person to calm down. Nothing useful comes from talking with someone too angry (or impaired by drugs, alcohol, or mental illness) to accept and drink a glass of water. Cheers!

If either of us failed the Drink of Water Test, it's not wise to ask the person why they hit you. If not, you can ask that in your head silently as to my motives. Ask yourself: "Why did you hit me?" This helps in determining your safety and to find solutions to our problem.

If we pass the Drink of Water Test, you can ask me, "Why did you hit me"?

⁂

Tantrum

[*Practicing the Three Levels of Anger*]

To master the Three Levels of Power, a little introspection and practice are required. The point of this practice exercise is to embrace the differences in:

- How it feels
- What we think
- What we do at each of the Three Levels of Anger

GOAL

The goal is to learn to move from Level Three to Level Two to Level One more easily. It's okay to go from Level Three to Level One if you can. Really, if we get to a true Level One once each day, it's a good start. Some days are harder than others.

Beware! When practicing the Three Levels of Anger… back away from your loved ones. Experience has taught me that it's best not to begin to practice this new response strategy and skill with relatives. They are so close to us, it's easier for us to go into automatic Level Three or Two modes.

When I first came to this country, my extended family came to our home almost every week for a Sunday meal. At one of these meals, some of the teens were speaking in their newly acquired English. They got into some silly stress-induced argument and suddenly one of them raised his voice, "And your feet stink!" I froze on the spot and tried so hard not to laugh but failed miserably. Soon, I noticed that the whole house was laughing so hard they could barely breathe. This totally childish Level Two response had transformed our family into a Level One spa of laughter.

To this day, we still say, "And your feet stink!" to end arguments.

Look to those golden moments.

Life provides many opportunities – anticipated and totally unexpected – in which to practice how much power we choose to keep and to give away. We have the option to contribute to a violent or grumpy world or to help foster a joyful, loving, generous world.

TANTRUM

One of my favorite You Tube videos is of a father and son in the grocery store. The boy wants candy and the father says, "No." The boy proceeds to have a huge screaming temper tantrum, throwing fruit off of shelves and throwing himself to the floor in full tantrum mode. Fellow shoppers look on.

At the end of the clip, the screen pops up with these words, "Use condoms." So I'm not a perfect Catholic, but it's funny.

Audiences laugh and laugh. Everyone can sympathize with this poor father and his son's plight. A public display of grand proportions does little to make any father or child feel in control and good about themselves.

LEVEL THREE: JERRY SPRING SHOW PARTICIPANT

"Jerry, Jerry, Jerry!"

If you were at Level Three, like a participant in the Jerry Springer Show, what could you do to make this situation worse? Remember, at Level Three your goal is to promote violence, attitude, and share grumpy moods.

When I ask audiences and patients this question I get an array of answers. I'd:

- Hit the boy
- Hit the dad
- Hand the dad my belt
- Yell louder
- Throw food
- Offer the dad a drink
- Video the scene and post it to Facebook
- Take the kid outside and give him a beating

You surrender your power and do nothing to contribute to the universe. You pass up on an opportunity to show grace, compassion and humor. Instead, you add pain.

LEVEL TWO: POLITE FOLK ANYWHERE

If you were at Level Two like typical Polite Folk, what could you do to surrender your power and not contribute positively to a compelling situation?

Audiences and patients say, I'd:

- Do nothing
- Give the dad that look, you know the one, a look of polite disdain
- Perhaps even "Tsk" with my tongue
- Give the boy that same look and a "Tsk"
- Leave the aisle or leave the store

And last but not least, my favorite, I'd:

- Give the boy the candy to shut him up. He's not my kid!

This is truly evil since it looks like a Level Two response but has a violent quality to it with its passive aggressive bent that speaks to a Jerry Springer Level Three response.

LEVEL ONE: YODA

"Ooooommmmm"

You are a sophisticated person with self-awareness, a conscientious attitude towards others and a sense of social justice. Your personal power is high and you live in grace, love, and gratitude, using humor and sophisticated communication skills in your daily life. This allows you to respond thoughtfully to most yucky situations.

QUESTION ONE OF THE FIRST LEVEL OF ANGER

In this situation, "Why did you hit me?" doesn't really apply. The real question is "What's happening here? Why is this happening?"

Audiences and patients say, I'd:

- See if the dad is okay
- See if he was drunk or drugged or experiencing low blood sugar
- See if the boy is okay, perhaps he is autistic and over stimulated by the noisy crowded grocery store
- See if the boy has low blood sugar or is having a seizure

QUESTION TWO OF THE FIRST LEVEL OF ANGER

How did I contribute to this? What do I need to do now?

Audiences and patients say, I'd:

- Tell the dad his kid has great vocal chords, could be an umpire, opera singer, etc.
- Give the dad a sympathetic look or smile
- Give the boy a sympathetic look or smile
- Tell the dad that it gets easier
- Get on the floor and scream and kick to distract the boy in a good-natured way
- Tell the boy to scream louder

"Tell the boy to scream louder." This last suggestion is referred to as prescribing the symptom. The thought is that if this child is out of control, asking him to scream louder or longer, which he is already doing, will cause him to have to revise his rebellious tactics. If the boy is listening, he can only continue to rebel by stopping the tantrum or getting quieter. Everyone wins.

How'd you do?

Now is a good time to think of a few situations that made you angry.

PRACTICE, PRACTICE, PRACTICE

Practice Level Three, Two, and One responses.

One fun and easy way to practice Level One responses is to first practice Level Three responses. These are deliciously inviting anyway. Besides, beginning practice with a worse-case response helps us clarify and recognize lost power and experience the joy of playing with wicked responses; letting off a bit of steam.

Remember to be kind and playful with yourself and others as you practice officially or on-the-spot of Yucky-Yummy events. Anything worth doing takes sustained effort.

ANOTHER PRACTICE SCENARIO

- Someone cuts into line in front of you after waiting at the airport security gate for 30 minutes. What would you do at?:
- Level Three
- Level Two
- Level One

As you practice, ask yourself:

- How did you do?
- What worked well? What didn't?
- What could you do to improve your response in the face of anger?

The Miami Wave

[*Practicing the Three Levels of Anger*]

I live in Miami. We have been voted–"the rudest drivers" in America, or is it the world? Anyway, our rude drivers are especially noteworthy.

Here's the scene that offers a chance to practice the Three Levels of Anger. As one of my kids used to say, "You see, what had happened was ..."

THAT SPECIAL SALUTE, THE MIAMI WAVE

One day, I was minding my business, driving on the Florida Ronald Reagan Turnpike heading south to Miami. I was going the speed limit in the middle lane. The nerve! How rude of me to drive within the speed limit. How inconvenient for everyone else!

A young man came up on my bumper very quickly. He became a hemorrhoid, tail gaiter and started to beep his horn for me to speed up. The faster left lane was blocked to him, as was the slower right lane. He was stuck and, suddenly, I was his problem. I was clearly making him late.

He expected me to oblige him, to fix his problem by speeding up to let him pass the cars on the left or the right. Imagine. Again, the nerve of me for going speed limit!

Then, he did it.

He did the Miami Wave, that special salute with one's middle finger, flashing it in his rear view mirror and later thrusting his manicured digit outside of his driver's window.

I started to get mad. Being a nice, middle-aged Roman Catholic Cuban-American grandma (or Lela – for abuela- as my grandchildren call me), I like to help young ones meet their goals, but not like this.

I thought about returning the special salute. My kids are shocked at this, but it entered my thoughts. It had a certain appeal at the moment. He had inspired my buffed middle finger to twitch.

POWER OF HUMOR AND GRACE

Then it hit me.

I could turn things around with a bit of humor and have some fun at his expense and mine. Really, the situation was ludicrous. So why not dive into the funny side of life.

I energetically raised my right hand in front of my rear-view mirror and gave him the friendliest, most welcoming wave I could, smiling and even jumping up and down in my seat a bit.

Much to my surprise, the young man returned my enthusiastic wave with a weak one. Yes, all of his fingers were involved in this wave. Outstanding!

Next, he backed off of my bumper and then let me in at a merger that was coming up. He could have sped up to pass me, cutting me off.

Maybe he thought I was his mother's friend, the preacher's wife, or his long-lost Aunt Betilda. Whatever the reason, he had become a perfect gentleman and citizen of the Miami roads. Ta da!

Since that day, I do this whenever I get the Miami Salute. I get a 65-75% return on my wave with a reciprocated wave.

Who knew that our response to violence could invite such immediate positive change? Okay, lots of people. I was just slow to catch up.

NOW ... WHY DID HE CHANGE HIS BEHAVIOR?

There are many answers to this. Three come to mind:

1. **Energy begets energy**
   I gave him humor, fun, and joy. It was contagious. Humor is even more contagious than a seriously grumpy mood.
2. **Guilt and shame**
   He might just have thought I was his long lost Aunt Betilda, the Preacher's wife, his neighbor, or his mother's friend.
3. **Natural goodness**
   People are eager to do the right thing, especially if invited to do so with grace and confidence. Had I been half-hearted in my wave, he might have interpreted that move as sarcastic.

Yes, smiles, humor, and positive energy are infectious and contagious. Try it out. It really works a good deal of the time.

⁂

Three Levels of Anger Worksheet

What are some possible responses at each Level of Anger?

Here's a worksheet to help you plan your responses to the anger in the three examples discussed thus far. We learn better when we are engaged in action. Active participation in problem solving also fosters Level One thoughts, words and deeds.

I invite you to write three possible responses for each of the Three Levels of Anger. Although this is hard work, keeping a playful sense of humor in mind helps us to be creative and to ward off shame and judgments that hinder the workings of our brain.

1. The Slap

THIRD LEVEL OF ANGER	SECOND LEVEL OF ANGER	FIRST LEVEL OF ANGER

2. The Tantrum

THIRD LEVEL OF ANGER	SECOND LEVEL OF ANGER	FIRST LEVEL OF ANGER

3. The Miami Wave

THIRD LEVEL OF ANGER	SECOND LEVEL OF ANGER	FIRST LEVEL OF ANGER

Beyond Blame, Shame and Lying

I've learned from every mistake I've made and from those that I avoided.
~ Anonymous ~ (*Millionaire Client*)

When we act poorly, shame and poor self-esteem are helpful self-correctors. One of my favorite actors is Cloris Leachman. Her character in the movie, *Spanglish*, said it best when her movie daughter was acting badly:

"Lately, your low self-esteem is just good common sense."

My father, Joseph N. Gurri, M.D. died when he was 94 years old. He was a wise, funny and practical man. When I felt guilty about something he would ask, "Are you guilty?" He noted the difference between feeling guilty and really being guilty. This always sobered me up into thinking about the facts and my responsibility.

Asking a question like this allowed me to find my own way out of my messes. Dad was not just a good dad and a good man; he was also a Freudian psychoanalyst and co-founder of the Florida Psychoanalytic Society. I know, can't you just smell the shrink's kid on me?

RESPONSIBLY IN ACTION: PUTTING GUILT TO GOOD WORK

When we find ourselves in a mess of our own making or created by others, three questions come to find to help sort out the issue of responsibility. These are:

1. **The seminal question is:**
   Who contributed to this situation?
2. **Secondly:**
   What did each participant contribute?
3. **Third:**
   What do we do about it now?

While many people interpret this as, Whose fault is this?, the real question goes beyond a basic level of morality, beyond blame and fear of punishment, to true acceptance of our power to contribute to even unlikely events.

***

Event Autopsies

{ *We all added to this mess!*
~ Jess Gurri Ennis ~
(*age 8*) }

When I was little, my siblings and I had the usual squabbles. My father, a real peace-lover, would be annoyed. He figured that we had come to this country for freedom and that we should be happy and safe.

"WE'RE A HAPPY FAMILY!"

He would shout, "We're a happy family!" This would always make us laugh. Just the thought of our tall, elegant father shouting about happiness would send us to giggles. Catching the humor of the situation, dad would wink at us, click his heals in the air and doff his huevo frito (those white canvas round hats that looked like huevo fritos or fried eggs) at us.

Making use of any event helps all of us achieve the peace and joy of life as true Level One responders.

EVENT AUTOPSIES

One way to truly accept responsibility in the practical and cosmic sense is to perform an Event Autopsy. Richard "Rick" Lavoie, M.A., M.Ed., is an educator who created Social Skills Autopsies as an exercise in self-awareness and accountability to help children with learning challenges.

Years ago, I discovered his videotape based on a book by the same name, Last One Picked, First One Picked On. I have morphed his Social Skills Autopsies into a more general concept of Event Autopsies and expanded his use of them over time.

An autopsy seeks to look to the underlying reasons for sickness and death. An Event Autopsy is a CSI (Crime Scene Investigation) inviting creativity, teamwork and responsibility for the greater good. If done well, it can be fun and informative.

GUILT-FREE AND SHAME-FREE ENVIRONMENTS

What I love about Event Autopsies is that they really invite accountability in guilt-free and shame-free environments. Without the lying or distortions fostered by a harsh evaluation of an event gone wrong, it's just so much easier to see things as they are. It's about simple curiosity and understanding.

Accepting responsibility can be exciting if we allow ourselves to see things from everyone's point of view. We are then free to problem solve for the next conflicted event.

Event Autopsies can be conducted in a fun way that affirms that we are each loved and that we do indeed love ourselves. It's about using reality in a 360-degree review of a situation with empathy and curiosity, only without the corporate angst.

Still, the truth is often painful - no matter how fun or light the approach.

CONFLICT HAPPENS

- Hmmm. How did I contribute to this?
- How did each of us in this situation contribute to the problem?

More importantly, we are then free to ask:

- What can I do now about it?
- What can I do next time to prevent problems or to make things go better?

Rules of the Event Autopsies

Hmmm. How did I contribute to this?
~ Margarita Gurri, Ph.D. ~

Here I fleshed out my experiences with the various audiences and patients who have played along with me using an Event Autopsy. It's just so much more fun and easy to get going if we look at even serious situations in a playful, light-spirited way.

GOAL

The goal is to establish a culture of discernment and stewardship. Event Autopsies teach us to problem solve, show compassion for others and ourselves - and think in socially responsible ways.

Can you imagine a world where we are all skilled and free to explore our choices in thought, word and deed?

I've established some ground rules to clarify expectations. Boundaries can be so very liberating.

EVENT AUTOPSY GROUND RULES

1. **Everyone Participates**
   - Each autopsy participant speaks to their own contribution first. They ask and answer the question: Hmmm. How did I contribute to this?
2. **Everyone Gives Feedback**
   - After everyone has spoken for him- or herself, each participant is invited to offer unseen or unspoken contributions on the part of other parties in a neutral, observational tone
   - How did each of us contribute to this situation?

3. **No Blame**
    - Chose an attitude of curiosity over blame
    - The point of an Event Autopsy is to invite self-awareness and other awareness
    - Accusations and self-blame block creativity and thoughtful brainstorming
4. **No Shame**
    - Shame is external, guilt is internal
    - Using shame as a primary tool in a gentle exploration of facts and responsibility truncates further discussion and self-awareness
    - Instead, invite exploration with curiosity and the excitement of self- and
5. **Feel free to ask, What can I do about it now?**
    - Here we really begin the brainstorming
    - Invite ridiculous options without editing
    - Then hone in on reasonable response options
    - Picking one or two options that can be implemented NOW!
6. **What can I do next time to prevent problems or to make things go better?**
    - Here is the heart of true learning
    - Anticipating future events and how to prevent them from happening or prevent them from escalating involves true learning about conflict, self and others
    - Self-care strategies are a key to this basic rule of Event Autopsies
    - If we are not relaxed, refreshed, well-fed, well-rested, with a plan to actualize our goals and values, how can we achieve a Level One life? We can't.
    - So, here is where we each examine our basic values, behavior and beliefs to create a life well lived

Toothpaste

Event Autopsy Practice:
"Hey! Where's my toothpaste?"
~ Margarita Gurri, Ph.D. ~

Here's an example created by Rick Lavoie and morphed by me as well as many Event Autopsy participants with whom I have worked and played.

You, Mary and I go to the same summer camp. We are all in the bathroom getting ready to brush our teeth after breakfast.

To make the telling of this story easier let's use these three people:

1. **Me**
2. **You**
3. **Mary**

ME

Being a supreme – and, of course modest - being, I bring my toothbrush and toothpaste.

Being less than stellar beings, you and Mary bring your toothbrushes but forget your toothpaste.

YOU

You ask me for my toothpaste, "Can I have your toothpaste?"

Being a generous sort, I say, "Sure" and hand you my toothpaste. I walk away, leaving the bathroom to join others having fun outside.

MARY

Mary then asks you, "Can I have your toothpaste?"

Also a generous sort, you say, "Sure" and hand over my toothpaste to Mary. You walk away to join the fun group outside.

THE CONFLICT

I see you and ask, "Hey! Where's my toothpaste?"

You shrug your shoulders and I am instantly angry.

So, who contributed what to this conflicted situation?

- Who?
- What?
- How?

Toothpaste Event Autopsy with Response Options

How did you each contribute to this mess?
~ Margarita Gurri, Ph.D. ~

When anyone has a conflict of any kind, it's a great opportunity to learn about ourselves, our power, and how we impact others.

It sometimes helps to learn with a facilitator, so let's pretend that Oprah, one of my all-time favorite humans, is helping us problem solve. Thanks, Oprah!

Oprah gathers the three of us and asks, "How did you each contribute to this mess?"

1. **Me**
2. **You**
3. **Mary**

"HOW DID I CONTRIBUTE TO THIS MESS?"

Most people respond by saying that someone else did something "wrong."

This isn't productive.

Instead, each person is invited to look at his or her own contribution to the situation. Rarely does the angry person start by looking at him or her. For kicks, let's start there.

ME, THE TOOTHPASTE OWNER

"How did I contribute to this mess?"

I can be sarcastic and say I was too generous. I can be shameful and blame you, saying that I shouldn't have trusted you. I can be mean and say that it's not my fault that you were irresponsible.

Or... I can look within myself and to the situation.

Audiences and patients say:

- I shouldn't have shared. Now. Is this really the point? Never a borrower or lender be?
- Nope. Also, it's easier to be creative if we stick to could have, instead of should have.
- Judgments can really narrow the brain when solving problems, in self-examination or exploring situational scenarios.
- I could have clarified expectations about the toothpaste. Did you think I was the Toothpaste Fairy giving away toothpaste to all in need? Perhaps I was a toothpaste heiress.
- I could have been clearer as to the terms of lending and borrowing.
- I could have squeezed off some toothpaste for you and left with my toothpaste in hand.

YOU, THE FIRST TOOTHPASTE BORROWER

"How did you contribute to this mess?"

Audiences and patients say:

- I could have clarified the terms for lending and borrowing.
- I should have asked if I could share your toothpaste with others. Again, let's avoid those thought-complicating "shoulds".
- I could have asked for just a bit of toothpaste and instead of taking the toothpaste container.
- It was a mistake to share your toothpaste with Mary. But was it? You're a generous soul. Of course you don't mind me sharing your toothpaste with someone else in need.

Rarely do you or any other person in your role think to say that:

- You didn't tell Mary that the toothpaste was mine so that Mary could thank me properly.

MARY

"How did you contribute to this mess?"

Audiences and patients say:

- I should have returned the toothpaste to you. How can you return toothpaste to the correct person if you didn't know who the real owner was?

- I didn't thank you for sharing
- I didn't ask you about expectations for sharing, borrowing or keeping

Rarely do you and Mary say:

- If I had brought my toothpaste, none of this would have happened.

Planning ahead and being prepared are often real ounces of prevention in the world of conflict and chaos.

Two Boys Fighting

Event Autopsy Practice: "How did I contribute to this mess? What are the solutions?"
~ Margarita Gurri, Ph.D. ~

Life offers many scenarios for practice.
Let's practice!

TWO BOYS FIGHTING SCENARIO

Yesterday, I witnessed two boys, ages 8 and 10, fighting over a video game in the grocery store freezer section. Their mom watched nearby, shaking her head; clearly frustrated, angry and embarrassed.

CHARACTERS

Once again, let's call these Event Autopsy participants: You, Mary and Me, just to make like simpler.

Oprah gathers the three participants and asks each to answer this golden question. For the sake of this example, let's assume that they are experienced and responsible Event Autopsy participants and we will go straight to Level One Yoda responses.

REMEMBER ...

The million dollar question is: How did I contribute to this mess?

YOU	ME	MARY
• I'm sorry I took your video game.	• I'm sorry I erased your game yesterday.	• Kids, what's happening here? • Who did what? • What can each of you do to fix this?

⁂

Event Autopsy Worksheet

How did each person contribute?
What can each person do now?
~ Margarita Gurri, Ph.D. ~

Here's a worksheet to help you execute a useful Event Autopsy. I've included space for possible solutions for each person on the path to conflict resolution.

1. Toothpaste

YOU	ME	MARY
Solutions?	Solutions?	Solutions?

2. Two Boys Fighting

YOU	ME	MARY
Solutions?	Solutions?	Solutions?

3. A Recent Event in Your Life

YOU	X	Y
Solutions?	Solutions?	Solutions?

BOOK II

TAO OF POO

Conflict as Invitations to Grace

> *Do you really want to be happy? You can begin by being appreciative of who you are and what you've got.*
> ~ Benjamin Hoff ~
> (*The Tao of Pooh*)

Many events in life contribute to our approach to conflict. Many pivotal events helped me to learn to use conflict as an invitation to grace. Two stories: One Less to Wash and The Red Shoe Story typify these.

"One Less to Wash."

For as long as I remember my parents took a positive view of life. Instead of complaining about losing their home, friends, and life in Cuba, they spoke of gratitude and freedom. They were true American patriots and practical in their faith and approach to crisis.

Other than what we wore and a suitcase full of possessions, we left all things behind in Cuba. We set up house in a small rented home between a cemetery and a firehouse. It was furnished with an orange sectional couch and one bathroom for all six of us. Friends and family helped each other and us. Someone always had what we needed.

One day, as I was helping to clean up breakfast dishes, I dropped one of our few glasses. It shattered all over the kitchen floor. I held my breath.

Grief-stricken, I figured my mother would be saddened. Instead, she came to me and said, "One less to wash." Together we cleaned up the shards.

RED SHOE STORY

Shortly after immigrating to this country, my mother took my twin sister, Elena, and me to a school picnic. Mom was elegantly dressed with beautiful red shoes. One grumpy and unwelcoming woman whispered loudly to my mother, "Pst, Beba ... Those shoes make you look loose." Although all these words were not yet part of our English vocabulary, the mean face made their meaning clear.

Mom paused, squared her shoulders, smiled and said, "Yes! I can dance." She did a little dance movement and floated along her path to greet other neighbors.

I'll never forget this. I was stunned and impressed. After seeing so many people fall apart with the changes in country, life status, culture, language and the resulting fears, anger, and regrets, it struck me that we really could make anything of a situation if we wanted. We were not stuck with unhappiness, not at the mercy of life events or others' reactions. Novel idea for me back then.

My mother's positive response to those unkind words changed my 4-year old world view forever. So, whenever I speak I wear red shoes as a nod to my parents' positive attitude and keen sense of humor. It is in those times of potential grumpiness and yuckiness that kids and adults learn most about how to respond emotionally and socially.

Tao of Poo

Things just happen in the right way, at the right time. At least when you let them, when you work with circumstances instead of saying, 'This isn't supposed to be happening this way,' and trying harder to make it happen some other way.

~ Benjamin Hoff ~

(*The Tao of Pooh*)

Years later, in Catholic Sunday School, I learned that my mother's approach matched that of the ancient philosophy of the Tao. From my understanding, the Tao is about embracing a life attitude that helps us maintain power in the face of yuckiness.

So, how do we do this? Where to begin…

The Tao of Poo is my simple take on the Tao Te Ching as it applies to parents and everyday life. I've tried to change this part as fitting for everyone, not just parents, but I kept this in for the sake of discussion – why improve on the Tao unless it is to focus it as a simple path for loving parents? Otherwise, why recreate the theory?

The Tao is literally the way or the path in Chinese language. It is attributed to sixth century philosopher Lao Tzu, or Old Sage. Events aren't good or bad, they just are.

It's all about what is.

Things seem good and bad, but really, they just are. Everything offers an opportunity for us to learn and to teach. It's up to us to use our experiences as opportunities to rise to any occasion, using yucky and yummy events and moods, ours and theirs, to shine. At our best, we flow with events while maintaining a grasp on our values, goals and personal power.

Poo happens. When talking to children, patients, first responders, military personnel and audiences about life's yuckiness, I created my own tongue-in-cheek version, the Tao of Poo.

I morphed the name from a book, The Tao of Pooh (as in Winnie the Pooh) by Benjamin Hoff. "Things just happen in the right way, at the right time. At least when you let them, when you work with circumstances instead of saying, 'This isn't supposed to be happening this way,' and trying harder to make it happen some other way." Instead of being crushed or artificially uplifted by events forever, we can use them as opportunities to rise to any occasion. We can use yucky and yummy events and moods, ours and theirs, to shine. At our best, we flow with the life's moments while maintaining a grasp on our values, goals, and personal power.

HENRY, "IT'S MINE! I'M KEEPING IT!"

A few years ago, a 4-year old boy, let's call him Henry, and his parents came to me for consultation. It seems that the boy had a problem poo-ing. He had been scoped, poked and probed by several renowned hospitals and experts in a series of very expensive comprehensive tests. Still no poo. No test can reveal motivation.

Finally, the family was sent to me, the shrink. When we met, I asked Henry a question any kid would think of, "Why don't you want to poo?"

Think for a moment of 4-year-old boys. What would they say?

Henry said, "It's mine! I'm keeping it!" To me he sounded like Bill Cosby during his comedy routines as he imitated children doing what children do. I laughed out loud. Henry laughed, too.

Henry's parents blanched. All this fuss, worry and expense over a normal, although exaggerated, response to individuation, or emerging independence, and control. To think that a kid could hold onto poo and anger so well.

Further discussion revealed that the boy wanted to keep his poo. It felt good inside but felt bad coming out, was messy and smelly. And besides, his 6-year-old sister would often rush to flush it, beating him in their race to pull the "flusher."

We talked about the wonders of poo. I told Henry that if he flushed his poo he would be one with the universe, feeding the flowers, grass and his beloved trees. Outside my office window are many trees, one of them had a big bumpy root that had tripped his sister as they walked on the grass before their appointment with me.

I pointed to the roots and told Henry that if he flushed a good poo, he could help these trees grow and help make these roots even bigger. The idea of tripping his sister gave Henry a new inspiration to poo and flush.

He asked if he could poo in my potty and went down the hall with his mother waiting nearby. A short while later, Henry emerged victorious. He rushed into my office, breathless to share the news.

"Dr. Margarita, I pooed! Wanna see it?"

Respectfully, I declined this offer that was enthusiastically accepted by his sister. They assure me that it was a "Dairy Queen swirly." Most impressive. I got a great big goodbye hug from Henry. I never saw them again.

TAO OF POO

Think of a yin and yang symbol with a Peter Griffin from Family Guy on one side letting go of everything and a 4-year-old boy on the other holding onto his poo, not wanting to let it go at all. Holding on and letting go are at the basis of Communication Aikido with the Three Levels of Anger, Tao of Poo and Polite Shut-ups.

The question is how to approach life's pleasant and not-so-pleasant that happenings in a way that to benefits loved ones, the community and us?

THE TAO OF POO AND STRESS

Before we go looking at conflict and Event Autopsies, it is important to acknowledge how stressful so many situations are for all of us.

We deal with our expectations, others' expectations and the perception of each of those. No wonder communication can be so stressful!

In dealing with stress and personal power, again the Tao of Poo comes in handy.

A graduate school classmate introduced the use of the Tao in the context of great stress to me; Lorraine Mangione, Ph.D. Lorraine was and is one of the most unique creatures I have ever encountered. She has an amazing spirit that allows her to cultivate friendship and cooperation in the most unlikely groups.

⁂

Three Choices when Faced with Stress

According to the Tao, we have three choices in any stressful situation. *We can:*

1. **Give In**
2. **Escape**
3. **Dive In**

GIVE IN

We can give in and:

- Just do what is easiest
- Do what others want us to do
- What our historical experiences tell us to do
- Hide behind culture and tradition
- Give up our voice solely to chains of command

Or:

- We can think and act for ourselves

If we give in, we just react. We are at the Third and Second Level of Anger and not in charge of our own selves. As my youngest daughter Kate used to say to her older sister, Jess, "You aren't the boss of me!"

Well, yes. I am the boss of you if you give me the power and react automatically to my anger.

ESCAPE

We can escape to:

- The land of make-believe
- Alcohol
- Other drugs
- Our favorite rationalizations
- Denial

In one of my favorite scenes from The Big Chill, Jeff Goldbloom's character says, "Rationalizations are more important than sex. When was the last time you went a whole day without a rationalization?"

We can avoid situations and create a rigid template, creating routines and procedures that are really bad escape habits.

We can blame:

- It's all my fault
- It's all their fault
- It's no one's fault
- It's everyone's fault

Or:

- We can dive in

DIVE IN

We can dive in with our eyes open and curiosity unfurled, allowing a genuine look at others, the situation and ourselves in context. This gets easier with practice. It can be thrilling to really problem solve effectively. We can look at our feelings and decide how to think and act, not just react to them.

What gets in the way?

Us! It's hard to love ourselves enough to know that it's okay to be flawed, to be wrong or to be immature from time to time. We all have reactions that would embarrass us if anyone could only know our thoughts and see us at our worst.

In the movie What Women Think, Mel Gibson is granted a magic gift/curse of being able to read women's thoughts; all women, all the time. How exhausting and how revealing. It's to his credit that he used this awareness of others to notice his own behavior and make some changes to his habits of the mind, spirit and behavior. It is his openness to diving in to his own self-awareness that makes him a better person.

So, let's dive in!

Three Choices Worksheet

Give it a whirl. I invite you to think of responses that fit each of the three choices you have for a crisis, disappointment or any other stressful situation you are facing now.

THREE CHOICES	EXAMPLES	YOUR RESPONSE
1. **Give In**	• Just do what is easiest • Do what others want us to do • What our historical experiences tell us to do • Hide behind culture and tradition • Give up our voice solely to chains of command	
2. **Escape**	• Fantasy land • Substance abuse • Rationalizations • Denials • Blame	
3. **Dive In**	• We can think and act for ourselves • Allow a genuine look at ourselves, others and the situation	

So, let's dive in!

Loss, Crisis and Humor

Humor is the great thing, the saving thing. The minute it crops up, all our irritations and resentments slip away and a sunny spirit takes their place.

~ Mark Twain ~

Many stories depict the possibilities of diving into loss and crisis with humor and grace. Here are a few examples.

MOMMY-DRESSED BOY AND GEOFFREY GIRAFFE

For some, not getting what they want or being able to give someone what they want feels like a crisis. Years ago, in Kansas City, Missouri, I was in a Toys R Us at the checkout counter. There was a mommy-dressed 4-year-old boy talking to his mother about this huge stuffed display of the Toys R Us mascot, Geoffrey Giraffe. The stuffed giraffe was almost as tall as the ceiling. Of course, I eavesdropped.

Boy: **"Mommy, I want him."**

Mom: **"Sorry honey. He belongs to the store."**

Boy: **"So, we can buy him."**

Mom: **"Then all of the other kids would be sad."**

Boy: **"They can visit our house."**

Mom: **"We couldn't get him home, he's too tall. We would have to rent a truck."**

Boy: **"Daddy has a truck."**

Mom: **"We'd have to cut a hole in our roof for him to fit."**

Boy: **"Okay."**

This went on and on with the frazzled and indulgent mother negotiating with so her son would not feel a loss. Wanting can be a treacherous or delicious thing. As we can see, the same goes for giving.

All she had to say was:

Mom: "Wow! Isn't he wonderful! Let's blow him a kiss. We'll see him the next time we're here. Bye, Geoffrey Giraffe!"

She hadn't grasped the notion that grief, little or big, is part of life. It's our job to learn to handle disappointments and loss in a way that adds meaning to the life of those we touch.

HUMOR AND LOSS

Whether the loss is small and a part of everyday disappointments or a devastating blow, the template for handling loss or change is the same. The key to handling loss is to be present to those little moments that help inform the bigger ones so that life is more livable and joyous. One great way of handling the stress of loss and change is humor.

"Humor is the great thing, the saving thing. The minute it crops up, all our irritations and resentments slip away and a sunny spirit takes their place." – Mark Twain

One of the funniest speakers I know is retired Navy Lt. Cmd. Charles "Chip" Lutz, president of Covenant Leadership. Since he introduced me to this quote, I always think of him when I see or say it. I guess you can say he gets stuck in my head! Chip would love the idea of his humor attaching itself to anyone who needs a dose of funny at any moment in time.

Comedy is often about mishaps and pain. Carol Burnett said that "Comedy is tragedy plus time."

In my youth I loved watching Carol and Tim Conway do skits. My favorite was Mrs. A-Wiggins, the excruciatingly slow receptionist secretary. My father would howl with glee. Watching him laugh was just as funny as watching the comedians enacting their craft. Laughter is just so deliciously contagious. This skit had us all laughing at Conway's stress and discomfort at the workplace when trying to use a new phone intercom with Burnett.

Why is it funny to see someone else experiencing stress in a skit? And why is it even funnier to see their reactions?

Of course, it's not so funny when it happens to us. Right?

⁂

Humor, Anger and Pain

Is your typical bowel movement …
Hugh?
~ Kennedy Krieger ~ (*Spine Clinic Intake Form*)

One of my family's favorite lines from Pretty Woman is when Richard Gere tells Julia Roberts, "I was very angry with my father." This is funny because they were in the bathtub at the time discussing anger and therapy. Roberts was listening to his tale of woe and comforting him in a funny way about her method of therapy, having her legs wrapped around him.

What's funny about being angry with one's father? Nothing.

What is funny is the context of anger, love, therapy, healing and a bathtub. Humor and laughter in context help us heal. Norman Cousins wrote extensively about the power of a positive attitude and mirth on the body's immune system, blood pressure, sugar regulation and ability to fend off many illnesses and respond well to treatment for various diseases. I recommend you read his Anatomy of an Illness (As Perceived by the Patient.)

THE STORY OF HUGH

When my daughter, Jess, broke her back in the fifth grade, our world stopped for just a bit. We went to Maryland's Kennedy Krieger Institute's Spine Clinic for an evaluation. Before this very stressful appointment, we had to fill out a "pile of forms," as Jess put it.

One of the questions had us roaring with laughter until we were crying and sputtering uselessly. The question was about poo. But of course, this is so appropriate for the Tao of Poo.

The question went something like this, "Is your typical bowel moment:"

1. **"Small like pebbles"**
2. **"Medium like rocks"**
3. **"Large like logs"**

Wait for it!

4. "Hugh" (instead of Huge)

Jess and I read this out loud together and stopped dead in our tracks.

"Hugh!"

Does some poo have a name now? This was hilarious. We roared.

The receptionist came over to see if we were okay. This sent us into further hysterics. We couldn't even talk. This was worse than someone farting in church. We could not contain our mirth.

To this day, we still tease about Hugh and find great comfort in the event. Humor, always our friend, had really pulled through for us on that momentous occasion.

By the way, Jess is okay. She has a bit of an interesting spine on the inside that looks so very strong and beautiful on the outside. The news we got that day was not as bad as feared or as good as hoped. Either way, she's fine and the mother of my youngest grandchild. Taryn Ennis, is now an amazing "almost three."

CONTEXT AND PERSPECTIVE ARE GOLDEN

Now, had this happened at any other time and place, we doubt that it would have been so funny. In a moment of crisis and pain, we found great comfort and humor in a simple typo.

Context is everything.

Communication Aikido with The Three Levels of Anger and The Tao of Poo is all about personal power in the face of anger, grief, fear and sadness. It's about the perspective we allow ourselves that invites personal power, grace and kindness.

BOOK III

POLITE SHUT-UPS

Polite Shut-ups

Our own sense of being, our personal power, is the most powerful Polite Shut-up as it can be a lovely pre-emptive strike, diverting much grumpiness from our path.
~ Margarita Gurri, Ph.D. ~

There are just too many grumpy people in the world. We all take turns being one of them, so let's look to some Polite Shut-ups that can help us limit our contribution to grumpiness.

Polite Shut-ups were created to keep my mind focused on humor and kindness when I was struggling with my temper. Children and adults have added to my ideas as we played with them. If you are tired of rude and want to set limits graciously, Polite Shut-ups are the answer. Polite Shut-ups are simple, fun limit-setting strategies that anyone can master. With a sense of humor, some communication skills and kindness, you can be a Master of Polite Shut-ups.

Conflicts within us and with others are inevitable. How we resolve these conflicts can deepen relationships and invite joy. On the other hand, how we resolve conflicts can cut us, or others, to the quick. I prefer to find gentle ways to move beyond conflicts. Life is so much better when choosing the high road.

THANKS TO MILITARY KIDS

It's been my privilege to work with many military families and children of all ages since my psychology clinical internship a long time ago. More recently, I've had the opportunity to support our American Military Personnel and their families as a member of the Department of Defense's Yellow Ribbon Program Speaker Cadre.

Kids have a way of seeking the most clear, concise solutions. Military kids especially, with their urgency and hard-won wisdom, have a way of making adults hone in on the real issues and solutions.

Because of them, Polite Shut-ups are "good to go" (as they say in the military) in a simplified format.

My sincere thanks to military kids from all branches of the United States Armed Forces for sharing their practical and often pressing need to laugh, communicate and connect with a parent or other loved ones during all phases of deployment. So, whether a loved one is getting ready to deploy, is already deployed or getting reading to return from deployment, military children have been my best teachers.

Seven Polite Shut-ups are introduced for your immediate use as strategies to summon and strengthen our personal power. They work effectively with just about anyone, anytime, when we are in any mood. All it takes is a little practice and some self-control.

We'll start with the hardest Polite Shut-up to master, Personal Power. It's hard to achieve, hard to maintain and hard to assess.

So, I offer some more thoughts on using our personal power and propose Seven Simple Polite Shut-ups.

Seven Simple Polite Shut-up Strategies

Look! There's the pope!
~ Daughter Jess ~
(As a teenager distracting us from a conflict)

Learning to use the Three Levels of Anger (or power in the face of anger) is a good start in dealing with anger and conflict. It's a great way to look at boundaries in terms of the possibilities in our own reactions.

How do you translate this into setting expectations and limits?

There are many ways. The idea of Polite Shut-ups came to me as I was struggling to teach patients and audiences strategies to handle others' anger using Level One responses. It's a fun way to practice. In workshops, we even practice this in the form of a Polite Shut-up Conga Line.

From the vast possibilities that exist as Polite Shut-ups, I've named seven for discussion. Of these, six lead up toward summoning, fostering and strengthening our personal power.

1. **Personal Power**
2. **Love**
3. **Gratitude**
4. **Accountability**
5. **Responsibility**
6. **Apology**
7. **Humor**

BASIC UNIVERSAL EMOTIONS

Although the Three Levels of Anger and Polite Shut-ups are presented here in the context of anger, the same principles apply to any emotion. Dr. David Matsumoto, a researcher of happiness and micro expressions, identified seven basic universal emotions.

Take a moment to guess what they are.

1. **Happy**
2. **Sad**
3. **Angry**
4. **Fear**
5. **Disgust**
6. **Surprise**
7. **Contempt**

So, as you read about the Polite Shut-ups, please keep in mind that the best way to shut someone up is to manage the situation beforehand; keeping in mind the basic emotions we can use to help set a proper tone for our purposes.

How do you set the tone?

Think about your expectations of others and situations.

Ask yourself:

- How do you let folks know what you expect?"
- Are you communicating effectively?
- Directly? Clearly? In a timely manner, with enough notice to allow everyone to think about and process your expectations and how to manage them.

Let's take a look at these Polite Shut-ups.

PERSONAL POWER

First of Seven Simple Polite Shut-ups Strategies

> *"It's annoying just how much of what we get back from others depends on what we invite."*
> ~ Margarita Gurri, Ph.D. ~

Personal Power is the most powerful Polite Shut-up. It's about being. Our own sense of being is the most powerful limit-setting strategy as it can be a lovely pre-emptive strike, diverting much grumpiness from our path.

THE POWER OF SELF-AWARENESS

What impact do you have on others?

A huge part of personal power is self-awareness. Unless we know how others perceive or misperceive us, how can we influence others with any strategy? We can't. There's just so much power in knowing ourselves.

Ages ago, I sparred in a Japanese martial arts class, mostly with men. One of many hard-earned lessons was to understand that most of my male sparring partners underestimated me because I am an average-sized woman. This knowledge became the basis of a great defensive and offensive strategy that allowed me to best more than one tall, strong, more accomplished martial artist. Like the song from School House Rock, "Knowledge is power."

Stop for a moment and just be.

How'd that go?

Usually, we are anchored to a variety of focal points: our loved ones, tasks that need doing, intrusive thoughts – such as joy, anger or anything else in the world around us.

DRAWING PERCEPTIONS: SENDING AND RECEIVING

When you were trying to just be, what did you send out? What did you receive?

We draw a response from others whether we want to or not. People really do respond, unconsciously and consciously, to us depending on our state of being.

Years ago, a grumpy patient of mine started to make great choices. He became a happy empowered man. One day, he shook his head and told me, “Isn’t it odd that now that I am happy, others seem happier, too?” It’s not just his perception.

It’s easier to see others’ feelings when we are in an attentive mode and tend to see what we are focused on. This is called Perceptual Vigilance. When you have a friend with a new red car, suddenly you are aware of all the red cars in your line of sight.

But this patient wasn’t noticing happiness just because of his perceptions. We draw responses from others whether we want to or not.

Test this long-established notion. Experiment with three different faces.

- Smile. Smile at the next few people you see.
- Neutral face. Then show them a neutral face.
- Unhappy face. Then an unhappy face.

Do they smile back more when you smile? Do you feel different? It’s annoying just how much of what we get back from others depends on what we invite.

OTHERS’ RESPONSES

Luckily, we do not have to be transcendent monks in order to exude calm and happiness. All we must do is still ourselves and send out love and other good intentions toward others. It seems we are hard-wired to respond to others’ feelings, intentions and energies.

We set limits with others and clarify expectations all the time, simply by being.

Next, I invite you to assess and strengthen your awareness of your own Personal Power. Then we will look at the other Polite Shut-ups.

Personal Power Awareness Exercise

[*Try it!*]

It's amazing! Just by mastering your own response to yourself and the universe, you draw a particular response from others.

Think of a recent interaction that comes to mind.

- How did you set the tone consciously and not so consciously?
- How did you set limits?
- How did you set expectations for yourself and for others?
- Was it verbal, non-verbal or both?

Try it!

1. Send out calm

Go to a crowded place like a grocery store, a busy street or the airport and just stand there. Draw yourself up to your full height and let your arms swing loosely in a relaxed stance. Be still. Send out love and calm. See how others react to you.

- Did they look at you?
- Quiet down?
- Smile at you?
- Send you guarded or grumpy looks?

2. Send out annoyance

Now try the same thing, only this time, summon your annoyance and agitation. How do people react now?

- Did they look at you? Look away?
- Quiet down? Speak to you?
- Smile at you?
- Get agitated?
- Send you guarded or grumpy looks?
- Did they avoid you?

3. Smile, look neutral, then unhappy

Smile at the next few people you see, then show them a neutral face, then an unhappy face. Do they smile back more when you smile?

- Do you feel different?
- Did they look at you?
- Quiet down?
- Smile at you? Avoid you?
- Send you guarded or grumpy looks?

It's annoying how much of what we get back from others depends on what we invite.

LOVE

Second of Seven Simple Polite Shut-ups Strategies

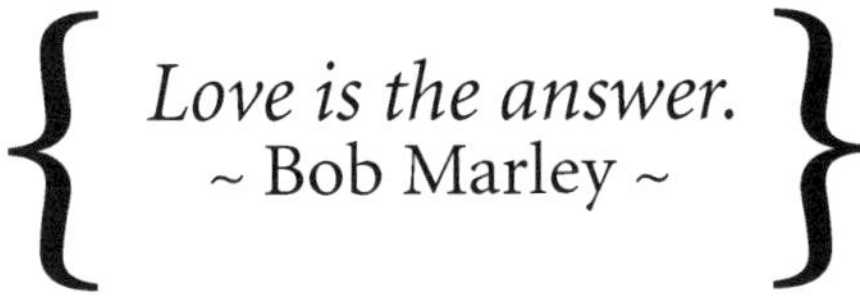

"I LOVE YOU."

Let's look at love.

Love is the second Polite Shut-up tool to help us retain and strengthen our Personal Power.

There are many types of love and ways to be loving. Handling a difficult interaction is one of them. Two stand out for me as particularly powerful in inviting conflict resolution: self-love and compassion for others.

What can be more important than love? One day, my friend Tony Palm, a retired Navy Chief Petty Officer, and I were talking about wounded warfighters and got into a discussion about love. Tony is President of Post Military Employment and works every day to find employment for our veterans.

Tony brings a practical warrior spirit with a fundamental perspective to his work with wounded warriors and recovering addicts. This tough guy speaks of love. In one of our recent brainstorming discussions on how to help military personnel and their families, he reminded me that there are many kinds of love. The Greeks embraced four basic types of love: Philos, Eros, Storge and Agape.

FOUR BASIC TYPES OF LOVE

1. **Philos**
2. **Eros**
3. **Storge**
4. **Agape**

- **Philos**

Philos is friendship love and includes the love we have for fellow human beings. It's about love for others. Philos in action is compassion.

- **Eros**

Eros is romantic, erotic or sexual love. It's the love we feel for a love match, a love or life partner. Quite different is sexual desire. Eros implies, in my way of thinking, that the love and sex with a beloved is for the one true love, not for the chosen sex partner of the day. Lust, although erotic, is not Eros, since it is not love at all. Eros transcends temporary, hormonal, pheromonal or need-based passion.

- **Storge**

Storge is familial love, it's about natural affection. It's the love of a parent for a child and a child for a parent and other kin or kindred spirits. In this way, it includes a special love between friends.

When old friends survive the passage of time, they are said to be blessed by Storge. We've all witnessed or experienced the sheer joy of meeting up with an old friend after a long break in continuity of active connection, maybe even years, and feel the immediate connection, as if time had not passed at all.

To confuse matters, Storge also includes lovers that started out as friends, and experience the survival of their connection whether or not they remain lovers. Either way, the main focus is the friendship and not the sex. It's about trust and caring.

- **Agape**

Last, but not least, is Agape. Agape is the love we have for God, for a greater power. It's unconditional love, an all-consuming forever kind of love.

To make love even more confusing, some believe that when we truly love a child, a mate or another human being, that it is truly Agape love, a Godly love.

BOTTOM LINE

When it comes right down to it, I believe that all four types of love identified by the Greeks are really two types of love: love for self and love for others.

To simplify for our simple model, I focus on love for self and others, viewing them as compassion for self and others.

- Compassion for Self
- Compassion for Others

How can you love another person without truly loving yourself? How can you love God without then loving yourself? They are all deliciously connected. It's about reciprocal love. All love flows both ways.

For people of faith, we believe that this affirms the presence of God and His love. For those who do not believe in a higher power, the practical applications of love remain compelling.

FOSTERING LOVE

As parents or professionals working with kids and parents, we devote ourselves to helping each child feel loved so that they can learn to love themselves and others.

This means that we give them the best that we have and unselfishly invite our children to love others fully. This can be difficult if the other person is a source of conflict for us, be it a relative, an ex-partner's new partner– the dreaded step-parent or someone who has been unkind to us.

By fostering love in the lives of our children, we invite them to be able to fully master Four Simple Tasks: Working, Playing, Giving and Receiving. The details of this are the topic of another book, The Five Elements. Below is a brief introduction into this paradigm.

THE FIVE ELEMENTS

The idea of Four Simple Tasks was expanded into an exercise when I was dealing with groups of military kids and adults who were having a very hard time connecting to others pre-, mid- or post-deployment. I tried these concepts out at a Department of Defense Yellow Ribbon Program for post-deployment soldiers, airmen and their families as an exercise in Self-care to foster reintegration.

The service members and families of one army group played along with the support of a brilliant, creative and strong leader, Lt. Col. Cynthia Rasmussen, Director of Psychological Health. Their openness in exploring their relationships to working, playing, giving and receiving created a demand for a new element that lent meaning, context and value to the entire paradigm.

The Four Simple Tasks had been morphed it into The Five Elements.

⁂

GRATITUDE

Third of Seven Simple Polite Shut-ups Strategies

"Receive graciously with gratitude. Ask for what you need. How else can others learn to be generous?"
~ Anonymous ~
(Family member, Department of Defense's Yellow Ribbon Program)

"THANK YOU."

"Receive graciously with gratitude. Ask for what you need. How else can others learn to be generous?" Anonymous family member, Department of Defense's Yellow Ribbon Program

Gratitude is the third Polite Shut-up. It is about acknowledging others' contributions to our lives in little and big ways.

Nothing can re-route an interaction more than gratitude. Whether you are appreciating someone or the fact that you two are connecting makes no difference. A good old-fashioned sincere "thank you" does wonders. Insincere thank yous just leave an ugly bad-smelling virtual puff of smoke in the air.

My favorite Army Chaplain, Lt. Col. Paul Crecelius, saves lives with his perspective. He has walked the walk and can talk the talk plainly. He is a humble, down-to-earth and funny man. The chaplain jokes that women are natural givers and men are natural takers. Although this is truly just a joke, it points out the importance of looking to our own basic natures, cultural upbringing and experiences to discern our true attitudes about gratitude and its requirement, receiving.

He speaks with gratitude of those good and not-so-good experiences that have fostered his faith, love and approach to life.

When I speak to really big audiences on Resilience, Self-care or Joyful Living, I sometimes have them do The Five Elements exercise.

ELEMENT ADVISORS

When I was playing with this paradigm, I consulted my friend and colleague, Ed Dunkelblau, Ph.D. Don't you just love his name? Anyway, Ed is the first friend I made as an adult in graduate school at the University of Kansas. We have remained dear friends. I love making him shake his head with my goofy sense of humor, so I often introduce him to audiences as "my oldest friend."

Anyway, Ed helped me play with how to introduce and structure the Four Simple Tasks and Five Elements exercise. As always, he is my steady go-to for anything having to do with Emotional Intelligence. He is a great problem solver with a sharp wit and a talent for making things simple and real. I'm not the only one that appreciates him as he was recently honored with a military appreciation award.

Back to The Five Elements ... I ask each warfighter and their loved ones at mid- and post-deployment Yellow Ribbon Program events to think about the five elements and name the one at which they are best. Since they are the best at one of the four elements, they are in essence, Element Advisors.

ELEMENT MOTTOS

Then, I split the participants up, sending each of the four self-chosen preferred element groups to sit at the tables near each of the four corners of the room. Each Element Advisory Group: Working, Playing, Giving and Receiving has five minutes to discuss the secrets of being good at their element. The task is for each group to create a motto that will inspire others to become better at their preferred element.

It is fun listening and observing each Element Advisory Group as they put their philosophy and advice into words that invite success.

What surprises me still is how few individuals in the audience will allow themselves to say that they are best at Receiving. At one event, a sophisticated woman was the only brave soul to identify receiving as her best element. As the only Element Advisor for Receiving, she came up with this most excellent motto.

"Receive graciously with gratitude. Ask for what you need. How else can others learn to be generous?" – Anonymous, audience Element Advisor Team, 2012

How can we be generous if we cannot receive? My mother once told me that if we never receive, not only do we not get anything but that we are acting in a stingy way. We are stingy because we prevent others from giving.

This flow of giving and receiving is a powerful Polite Shut-up. It summons personal power in all persons involved in a conflict. Whether each person answers this call to a strengthened being is a personal choice made by each of us each moment.

CORRECTIVE ACTION

Fourth of Seven Simple Polite Shut-ups Strategies

[*I'll get right on that.*]

Corrective Action is the fourth Polite Shut-up. Nothing stops a conflict quicker than a genuine statement of corrective action. This is accountability and reliability rolled into one. Sexy stuff. We are all awed by what should be commonplace: doing what they were and are supposed to do. No fanfare. Just correct action.

One of the main reasons for conflict in any situation and relationship is that someone did not do what they said they would do, when and how they said they would do it. We can avoid any further conflict by stating that we will "get right on that." Problem solved. Kind of.

Completing an undone task resolves the content of the dilemma. It does not resolve the fact that we did not do what we committed to do in a timely or sufficient manner. This aspect of the Polite Shut-up can be resolved with a swift Apology as discussed in one of the Polite Shut-ups.

RESPONSIBILITY

Fifth of Seven Simple Polite Shut-ups Strategies

Who doesn't love to hear those words? Taking full responsibility for our direct and indirect contributions to any situation is the fifth Polite Shut-up. Respect requires us to take full responsibility.

It's about what we say and don't say, do and don't do, think and don't think, and feel and don't feel. It's a full accountability of the short- and long-range consequences of our actions.

We all know that every moment is pregnant with abstinence. Each moment comes with a choice to do or not do something.

When we are facing potential conflict, nothing works faster than to reframe and defuse the situation than to say or hear, "You're right." Conflict ends right there unless a hidden agenda remains.

APOLOGY

Sixth of Seven Simple Polite Shut-ups Strategies

{ *Never ruin an apology with an excuse.*
~ Kimberly Johnson ~ }

"I'M SORRY!"

Those words stick in our throats so often. Because of this, a simple, well-done apology is the sixth Polite Shut-up.

One, two, three… "I'm sorry!"

When my daughters Jess Ennis and Kate Gurri Glass were little, I overhead them apologizing to each other in a not-so-apologetic manner, "I'm sorry you made me hit you." As always, they made me laugh.

Sometimes apologies need a little help. I used to have my kids apologize to each other on the count of three. It is important to make good use of life's opportunities to apologize as one of the saving graces of each and every mistake we make, they make, others make. Apologies are great teachable moments for character, values, choices, behavior and forgiveness. They put anger to good use.

We forget the power of a true apology. After all, an apology is about accepting full responsibility for our power in a relationship's difficult moments.

A true apology is sincere and has at least three components. The hard part is to match the apology to the offense. If we over-do the apology, the aggrieved owes a debt. If we under-do an apology, we owe a debt. A true apology wipes the slate clean in terms of debt.

APOLOGIES

No one likes to apologize.

Lucky for us, we all make mistakes frequently and have a great many opportunities to learn from them and to practice the art of the apology. Here's the catch. We can only learn from mistakes if we acknowledge them, take responsibility and make amends with ourselves or others.

Apologies can be a complicated philosophical and spiritual exercise. For me, they are a simple, practical Action Path. "An apology is the superglue of life. It can repair just about anything." – Lynn Johnston, Canadian cartoonist, *For Better or For Worse.*

MISTAKES AS TEACHABLE MOMENTS

Mistakes can be great teachable moments. Just about any relationship can be made stronger with the cycle of offense, apology and forgiveness. A good misunderstanding or thoughtless word or deed can do great harm. The apology that follows can do great good. The Forgiveness that follows that can seal mutual trust and respect.

Let's delve into the Art of the Apology with Forgiveness below.

Art of the Apology with Forgiveness

"I'm sorry" and "I forgive you."
(Any pair apologizing successfully)

What good are the Three Levels of Anger and Event Autopsies if we don't know the Art of the Apology with Forgiveness? A Five-step Recipe for a Good Apology is offered.

FIVE-STEP RECIPE FOR A GOOD APOLOGY: "NMM"

"NMM" is a pneumonic device that matches the first letters of the first three steps of an apology and mimics the sound that we make when we are stammering to come up with the words that form an apology. It got its name from an adjudicated youth with whom I worked.

APOLOGY STEP	EXAMPLE	THE TASK
1. **Step One** N: Name the offense	"I'm sorry I borrowed your toothpaste, shared it with Mary and did not tell her it was yours and failed to return it to you."	Name the thing that you did, fully. Action plus feeling.
2. **Step Two** M: Make a promise	"I promise to not share your possessions with others without your permission."	Make a promise to not do the thing again.

APOLOGY STEP	EXAMPLE	THE TASK
3. **Step Three** M: Mitzvah or make amends	"I will tell Mary that the toothpaste I lent her was yours so she can thank you. Here is a brand new toothpaste tube to replace the one you lent me. I'll keep the used toothpaste that Mary still has."	Mitzvah time! Or make amends. Wax on and wax off. Slam the door. Sing. Hit. Kiss. Break. Fix and kiss.
4. **Step Four** Forgiveness	"I forgive you."	The apology is accepted by the offended one.
5. **Step Five** The apology acceptance is acknowledged and appreciated by the offending one.	"Thank you."	If the offense is repeated, the apology is not a real apology.

FIVE-STEP RECIPE FOR A GOOD APOLOGY: "NMM"

1. **Step One, N:**
   NAME THE OFFENSE
   - Name the thing that you did, fully. Action plus feeling.
   - "I'm sorry I borrowed your toothpaste, shared it with Mary and did not tell her it was yours, and failed to return it to you."
2. **Step Two, M:**
   MAKE A PROMISE
   - Make a promise to not do the thing again. For families that do not believe in promises or oaths, to try not to do the thing again.
   - "I promise to not share your possessions with others without your permission."

3. **Step Three, M:**
   MITZVAH OR MAKE AMENDS
   - Mitzvah time! Or make amends. Wax on and wax off. Slam the door. Sing. Hit. Kiss. Break. Fix and kiss.
   - "I will tell Mary that the toothpaste I lent her was yours so she can thank you. Here is a brand new toothpaste to replace the one you lent me. I'll keep the used toothpaste that Mary still has."
4. **Step Four:**
   FORGIVENESS
   - The apology is accepted by the offended one.
   - "I forgive you."
5. **Step Five:**
   THE APOLOGY ACCEPTANCE IS ACKNOWLEDGED AND APPRECIATED BY THE OFFENDING ONE
   - If the offense is repeated, the apology is not a real apology.
   - "Thank you."

CRITICAL FEATURES OF A REAL APOLOGY

A real apology is:

- Genuine
- Avoids blaming the person, takes full responsibility
- Demonstrates full understanding of the offense
- How the offense affected the other person
- Not a springboard to other complaints or accusations

Apology Worksheet

I'm sorry that you were such a baby that you had to go and tell mom.
~ Daughters Jess and Kate ~
(as kids)

Apologies get easier with practice. Below is a worksheet inviting you to practice the Five-step Recipe for a Good Apology.

Remember that a real apology is:

- Genuine
- Avoids blaming the person, takes full responsibility
- Demonstrates full understanding of the offense
- Clear about how the offense affected the other person
- Not a springboard to other complaints or accusations

APOLOGY WORKSHEET

APOLOGY STEP	THE TASK	YOUR RESPONSE
1. **Step One** N: Name the offense	Name the thing that you did, fully. Action plus feeling.	1.
2. **Step Two** M: Make a promise	Make a promise to not do the thing again.	2.
3. **Step Three** M: Mitzvah or make amends	Mitzvah time! Or make amends.	3.

APOLOGY STEP	THE TASK	YOUR RESPONSE
4. **Step Four** Forgiveness	The apology is accepted by the offended one.	4.
5. **Step Five** The apology acceptance is acknowledged and appreciated by the offending one.	If the offense is repeated, the apology is not a real apology.	5.

Adventures in Apologies

I'm sorry but you made me yell!
~ Daughters Jess and Kate ~
(as kids)

We can only learn from mistakes if we acknowledge them, take responsibility for them and make amends with ourselves or others. I invite you to be adventurous in an introspective way. Self-awareness is almost never easy.

YOUR LAST APOLOGY

Think of the last apology you made to someone.

1. **What happened and how did you handle it?**
2. **What did you say?**
3. **How did you do?**
4. **Did you follow the recipe for a real apology?**
5. **Did you follow the guidelines for a real apology?**

How'd you do?

Did you do the full "NMM" and hit all the features of a real apology? Please reference the pages before this one to make sure your apology was genuine and complete enough to earn forgiveness from yourself and the offended one.

THE LAST APOLOGY THAT YOU RECEIVED

Now, think of the last apology someone made to you. That you received.

1. **What happened and how did you handle it?**
2. **What did you say?**
3. **How did you do?**
4. **Did you follow the recipe for a real apology?**
5. **Did you follow the guidelines for a real apology?**

How'd you do?

Were you gracious? Did you help the apologizer by making sure that the offense was properly noted out loud with all its elements? If not, how can you truly accept an apology? How can forgiveness take root?

HUMOR

Seventh of Seven Simple Polite Shut-ups Strategies

Hey, how's your fingah?
~ Elena Gurri and husband Larry Levis ~

"LET ME TALK!"

Last but not least, the seventh Polite Shut-up is humor with a light-hearted spirit, also known as Connie's Solution.

CONNIE'S SOLUTION

Last year, I was giving a keynote at a Yellow Ribbon Program post-deployment event for soldiers and airmen who had returned from Afghanistan. The soldiers and airmen, their families and commanders were in a beautiful hotel ballroom preparing to listen to lots of briefs about their benefits and available resources.

Feelings were definitely mixed about being there for a weekend so soon after their return to their families and the United States. The idea of sitting inside all day, away from home, listening to briefs and watching PowerPoint Presentations can make the bravest service member weak at the knees.

It was my job to warm them up and set a tone for interest and involvement. I dove into Communication Aikido. During my talk, a table in the back drew my attention. There were raised angry and laughing voices. After my talk, I just had to investigate. There was a lovely couple fighting about something.

I asked the tablemates how they were. The husband rolled his eyes at me and his wife. He explained that his wife was angry with him. Apparently, he was talking and teasing his tablemates the whole time I was talking. I laughed since the goal of these events is to get folks communicating among themselves and various service providers. The wife wanted to listen to me deliver my keynote and was annoyed with her husband's playfully disruptive approach to the day's events.

Anyhow, when the wife, Connie, tried to talk to her husband about her annoyance she intended to say, "Would you shut up and let me listen?"

Instead, out came, "Let me talk!"

The husband thought this was funny. This made Connie even more annoyed and frustrated. It didn't help that the other soldiers at the table were chuckling at the pair.

Luckily, the couple graciously allowed me to use this incident as an example of how something that is not funny can be used later as an endearing and humorous Polite Shut-up. Although she remained embarrassed, I thought this beautiful wife was brilliant.

"HEY, HOW'S YOUR FINGAH?"

When my twin sister and her longtime husband were newlyweds, they had a fight. It was one of those silly ones with big emotion. One of them had a broken finger in a splint.

Suddenly, the other one said in a playfully thick New York accent, "Hey, how's your fingah?"

They both laughed and the fight ended. Since then, all they have to do is ask, "Hey, how's your fingah?" and most tiffs are happily dispatched.

Polite Shut-ups Worksheet

Practice each of the seven Polite Shut-up strategies

Here's a worksheet to help you practice. Intentional practice helps us build a template that prepares us for gracious polite shut-ups in most any situation.

Someone not that close to you asks:

- "Can I borrow $1,000?" or they ask an intrusive question:
- "Have you had an affair?"
- "An STD?"

POLITE SHUT-UPS WORKSHEET

POLITE SHUT-UP	YOUR RESPONSE
1. **Personal Power**	
2. **Love**	
3. **Gratitude**	
4. **Accountability**	

POLITE SHUT-UP	YOUR RESPONSE
5. Responsibility	
6. Apology	
7. Humor	

Personal Action Plan

You must be the change you want to see in the world.
~ Mahatma Gandhi ~

To really communicate, we must continually be self-aware.

I learned a long time ago that if we commit to doing something, say it out loud to someone or put it in writing; we are more likely to follow through with our goals. It's about accountability and about taking the time to craft our goals more carefully since we will be sharing them.

What is one thing you can do - today, this week, this month - to become more aware of what you do with your power in the face of someone's anger and invite Level One choices.

It might help to do this if you take a moment to reflect on:

- The Three Levels of Anger
- Event Autopsies
- Tao of Poo
- Polite Shut-ups
- The Art of the Apology with Forgiveness

ASK YOURSELF

WHAT'S MY GOAL?	TO WHOM WILL I TELL MY GOAL?	WHAT'S MY PERSONAL ACTION PLAN?

⁂

Biography

By Steve Lee

Dr. Gurri is a licensed psychologist who for years has educated and motivated leaders and families, military personnel and couples, parents and youth alike. For her it's all about honest, effective communication and strengthening relationships.

With a proven track record as a consultant, international speaker and author, Dr. Gurri's unique approach is tinged with a bit of humor, sprinkled with plenty of anecdotes and brimming with optimism that stem from, not only her keen insight but her personal and professional experiences as well.

Dr. Gurri has 30 years of experience in the field. She earned a Ph. D. in clinical psychology at the University of Kansas and completed post-graduate work at the University of Maryland and Menninger Institute.

Among her numerous affiliations are: American Psychological Association; Association for Applied and Therapeutic Humor; Florida Psychoanalytical Society; Florida Psychological Association; Florida Speakers Association, Latin America and National Speakers Associations; and the Department of Defense Yellow Ribbon Speaker Cadre.

Resources and References

Cousins, Norma, *Anatomy of an Illness As Perceived by the Patient.* Bantam, 1991.

Donovan, Frank, MAASW, *Dealing with Your Anger.* Hunter House Publishing, 2001.

Hoff, Benjamin, *The Tao of Pooh.* Penguin Books, 1983.

Johnston, Lynn, *For Better or For Worse.* Universal Press Syndicate, Andrews McMeel Publishing, 1997-2004. **fborfw.com**

Lavoie, Rick, M.A., M.Ed. *Last One Picked, First One Picked On.* DVD, **RickLavoie.com**

Matsumoto, David, Ph.D. Researcher and speaker on happiness and micro-expressions. **DavidMatsumoto.com**

Ruiz, Don Miguel, *The Four Agreements: A Practical Guide to Personal Freedom.* (A Toltec Wisdom Book.) Amber-Allen Publishing, 1977.

Tsu, Lao, *Tao Te Ching.* Translated by Gia-Fu Feng and Jane English, Vintage Books, 1997.

17098545R00069

Made in the USA
Charleston, SC
26 January 2013